Original title:
Laughing My Way to Enlightenment

Copyright © 2025 Creative Arts Management OÜ
All rights reserved.

Author: Sophia Kingsley
ISBN HARDBACK: 978-1-80566-245-7
ISBN PAPERBACK: 978-1-80566-540-3

The Lightness of Being

In a world where misunderstandings bloom,
We trip on thoughts, not doom and gloom.
A whisper of hope with a wink so bright,
We dance through the chaos, in pure delight.

Each stumble a giggle, each fumble a cheer,
We toast to the joy lurking near.
With every small blunder, we find our grace,
The mirror reflects our silly face.

Giggles in the Garden of Wisdom

In the garden where musings sprout,
We chase after truths, without a doubt.
A flower of folly, a petal of jest,
In the soil of laughter, we find our rest.

With each giggle shared, wisdom takes flight,
The bees buzz with joy, what a delightful sight!
Under the sun, where we play and sway,
We harvest the smiles that brighten our day.

The Serendipity of Smiles

Stumbling upon laughter, what a sweet fate,
In moments of blunder, we celebrate.
A twinkle of joy, like stars up above,
Bringing hearts together, like hand fits glove.

With a wink and a nudge, we leap into cheer,
As silly slips fate, it's all oh so clear.
Every snicker's a treasure, every snort a gem,
Life's comedy unfolds, we're laughing with them.

Dance of the Jovial Spirits

In the moonlight glow, spirits frolic and play,
Twisting and turning, they dance away.
With chuckles that echo through the trees so tall,
In the rhythm of joy, we sway and we sprawl.

They tell stories of mishaps, of blunders so grand,
In this whimsical world, we take a stand.
With every giggle, the night comes alive,
In the dance of joy, we thrive and we jive.

Finding Clarity in Comedic Moments

In the swirl of laughter bright,
I stumble through the day and night.
With every chuckle, wisdom peeks,
And nonsense, oh, how often speaks!

A joke about the moon's big cheese,
Brings insight greater than you'd seize.
In every giggle, truth unfolds,
A dance of wit, and joy consoles.

Laughing Shadows of the Past

In shadows cast by silly dreams,
I find the laughter springs and beams.
Those awkward moments, oh so bright,
Transforming blunders into light.

A slip, a trip, a fall from grace,
Each folly wears a smiling face.
The past, it grins like an old friend,
And every fumble knows no end.

The Joyful Echo of the Heart

When giggles bounce upon my chest,
I find a warmth, a playful jest.
The echoes of a hearty cheer,
Remind me that the world is clear.

With every pun, my spirit soars,
As laughter opens all the doors.
A joyful heart, it beats so true,
In every chuckle, skies turn blue.

Riddles Wrapped in Laughter

In riddles wrapped in laughter tight,
I seek the puzzle day and night.
What's heavy as a mountain yet
Can lift the soul without a sweat?

A riddle weaves through giggles bright,
Where questions dance in pure delight.
With every answer, joy expands,
And wisdom plays in playful hands.

When Laughter Becomes a Guide

In a world so serious, we dance,
Let humor lead, it's our chance.
With giggles as our trusty map,
We stumble, we trip, then we clap.

Jokes floating like bubbles in air,
Tickling sides, we cast out despair.
Each chuckle a step on the way,
Guiding us gently, come what may.

Illuminated by Kindred Chuckles

Under the glow of silly puns,
United we stand, a band of funs.
With snorts and wheezes, our hearts ignite,
Together we shine, oh what a sight!

In the circle of jesters, wisdom blooms,
Each laugh a petal in joyful plumes.
We share our quirks, our quirks we adore,
In our colorful world, there's always more.

Hilarity Among the Stars

The cosmos grins, a winking star,
While comets race with jokes from afar.
Galaxies swirl in a dance so bright,
Tickled by cosmic delight.

Floating on giggles, we drift through space,
Waves of laughter, a warm embrace.
Planets spin in a joyful jest,
In this universe, we're truly blessed.

The Wisdom of a Playful Heart

A heart that dances, a merry beat,
With every tumble, we find our feet.
Silly mistakes make the best of tales,
As wisdom rides on laughter's sails.

In a world of seriousness, we find,
The simple joys, so unconfined.
With a wink and a laugh, we start anew,
A playful heart sees the world askew.

A Symphony of Smirks

In the hall of giggles bright,
Wisdom winks with sheer delight.
Chasing clouds of silly dreams,
I find truth in joyful screams.

Every chuckle has a tale,
Of life's folly, light as ale.
Jesters dance on thoughts so grand,
With a wink and silly hand.

Laughter's potion, sweet and pure,
Opens hearts, the spirit's cure.
In the rhythm of the jest,
I discover life's true zest.

So come and join this playful spree,
Enlightenment, a cup of tea.
Raise your glass with a twinkling eye,
As we toast to the reasons why.

The Mirthful Muse

The muse appears in a bright hat,
With a grin and a cheeky spat.
She juggles thoughts like playful balls,
In the land where humor calls.

Each pun is a moonbeam's flight,
Dancing softly in the night.
Giggling shadows beneath the trees,
Whispering secrets on the breeze.

In the canvas of babe laughs,
Life's absurd at every half.
With a tickle and a tease,
Truth reveals in joyous breezes.

Drink deep from this well of glee,
And let go of solemnity.
Embrace the fun in life's routine,
And find delight in the serene.

Follies of Enlightening Encounters

In the park where wisdom plays,
Silly moments fill the days.
A stumble here, a goofy fall,
Life's lessons come with a call.

The wise old sage with shoes untied,
Laughs aloud, no need to hide.
He shares his tales with a wink,
In the silly side of life, we think.

Each blunder wraps a secret gleam,
In folly, we find our dream.
The universe jokes, it's true,
With every slip, we start anew.

So bring forth your joyful grin,
Let this light-hearted dance begin.
For in the laughter's embrace,
The path reveals its wondrous grace.

Wisps of Wisdom and Whimsy

On the road paved with delight,
Whimsical thoughts take to flight.
Like butterflies, hope dances free,
In the chaos, find a key.

Sipping tea with a playful twist,
Life's lessons oft get missed.
But with a sigh and giggle loud,
Wisdom hides beneath a cloud.

Ride the waves of laughter's tide,
With every grin, our hearts collide.
A fool's parade, the wise will cheer,
In this silly, boundless sphere.

So let your spirit bubble up,
In the joy, we fill the cup.
With wisps of whimsy and a jest,
We find the truth that brings us zest.

Glimmers of Insight in Glee

In a world so bright and bizarre,
Wisdom hides like a shooting star.
With every chuckle, thoughts unfold,
Jokes become stories, tales untold.

Dancing through mind's tangled maze,
Laughter leads in curious ways.
Each giggle, a new truth to find,
Unlocking treasures in the mind.

Witty quips and funny faces,
Reveal life's most peculiar places.
Through humor's lens, we clearly see,
Life's deeper meaning, wild and free.

Finding the Divine in the Droll

Sandwiched between the whimsy and the wise,
Divinity waits in clever disguise.
A pun, a jest, a playful glint,
Reveals the essence in every hint.

With giggles echoing through the halls,
Insight comes when laughter calls.
Every chuckle opens a door,
To wisdom resting on the floor.

Silliness dances in sunlit beams,
In joyous moments, we dare to dream.
Through each playful jest, we unearth,
The sacred joy, our congregated mirth.

Frolics in the Land of Knowing

In a realm where smiles abound,
Knowledge frolics all around.
Chasing rainbows, spinning tales,
The heart of wisdom never fails.

Cracking jokes with glee, we find,
Truths that slip through the grind.
Every folly, every slip,
Turns the mundane into a trip.

With thoughts as light as balloons in the sky,
We lift the spirit, let it fly.
In laughter's dance, secrets unfold,
Lessons wrapped in humor's gold.

Secrets Beneath Joyful Masks

Masks of laughter hide the wise,
Behind each grin, a new surprise.
Jokes like treasure maps, we roam,
In playful banter, we find our home.

With quirky quirks and silly schemes,
We unravel life's most tangled dreams.
Each giggle holds a spark of light,
Guiding us through the starry night.

Peeling layers of laughter's crest,
We discover truths that never rest.
Beneath the jests, we learn to see,
Life's greatest secrets, wild and free.

The Art of Lively Reflection

In the mirror, a jester grins,
Wiggles and wobbles, where it begins.
With every chuckle, a truth is spun,
Finding joy in the silly run.

Each thought a balloon, floating high,
Dancing on whims, soaring sky.
The world's a stage, a playful play,
Where seriousness fades, and giggles stay.

Wisdom wears a funny hat,
Tickles the mind, like a clever cat.
In the riddle of laughter, light does gleam,
Reflecting a life that's truly a dream.

With silly dances and quirky moves,
We embrace the life that constantly grooves.
So let's twirl 'round in this playful glee,
In this artful dance, we are truly free.

Embracing the Absurdity of Being

Lions in pajamas, oh what a sight,
Roaring with laughter, day turns to night.
Tiptoeing softly on the edge of sane,
Life's bizarre twists are our greatest gain.

In the land of strange, where socks don't match,
We giggle at fate, what a splendid catch!
The cosmic joke, a grand old scheme,
Tickling the heart, igniting the dream.

Twisting truths into silly shapes,
A parade of quirks, the mind escapes.
Embracing the jest, with open arms,
Finding delight in life's funny charms.

With a wink and a nod, we join the dance,
Laughing at life, it's all pure chance.
In the absurd, we play and sway,
Finding joy in the light of day.

Sunshine Through the Cracks

Through cracks in the pavement, light bursts through,
Little rays of joy, breaking the blue.
A giggle escapes as shadows retreat,
Sunshine and laughter create perfect heat.

Creaky doors open, a squeaky song,
Silliness in moments where we belong.
Beams of delight in the oddest of places,
Joy shines brightest on funny faces.

Fleeting clouds toss their worries away,
Laughter emerges, come what may.
In the dance of sunbeams, we sway with ease,
Finding bright treasures, like whimsical keys.

With a chuckle and cheer, the day sees light,
We shuffle and jiggle, from morn until night.
In every crack, let the joy unfold,
Sunshine so sweet, bright stories told.

Silly Secrets of the Mind

In the attic of thoughts, a parade begins,
Silly little whispers, spinning like spins.
With a wink of delight and a dash of glee,
Secrets emerge, wild and carefree.

A riddle or two, they fly on a kite,
Soaring through clouds, what a wondrous sight!
In the tomfoolery, wisdom finds way,
Silly tricks turn the night into day.

Ticklish thoughts dance 'round like a breeze,
Lifting the spirits with such simple ease.
Silly jests lined in our brain's cozy nook,
Turn troubled pages into a happy book.

With laughter as fuel, the mind takes flight,
Exploring the joys hidden in plain sight.
In every secret, a giggle resides,
Unlocking the doors where fun always hides.

The Lightness of Grins

With a tickle in my heart, I glide,
Each giggle a wave, a joyful ride.
Banter like bubbles, they rise and spin,
In this frothy dance, let the fun begin.

Laughter like candy, sweet and bright,
Chasing shadows away with delight.
In this playful breeze, I sway and twirl,
Sailing on smiles, as the echoes unfurl.

Giggling Through the Cosmos

Stars wink down with a cheeky grin,
Galaxies twirl in a cheeky spin.
I float through space on a chuckle's breeze,
Finding joy in the cosmic tease.

Planets burst forth with a comical show,
As comets zoom by with a jovial glow.
In this vast playground, I learn to play,
Giggling softly, swirling on my way.

Chuckles Beneath the Stars

Under the canopy of diamond light,
Whispers of laughter bloom in the night.
Moonbeams giggle in the silver air,
Creating moments that are truly rare.

I skip over puddles made of joy,
In each reflection, a gleeful ploy.
The universe grins at this caper of mine,
Illuminating paths where the stars align.

Joyful Journeys to Clarity

With a skip in my step and a grin so wide,
I wander the paths where the happy abide.
Sunshine and giggles dance all around,
In each playful moment, new wisdom is found.

Traveling lightly, I juggle each thought,
Learning from laughter, it's joy that I've sought.
Adventure awaits in each silly turn,
The light of my heart is forever to burn.

Sunshine on the Path of Understanding

Chasing shadows with a grin,
Bright ideas dance within.
Who knew wisdom wore a hat?
A jester's joke, a friendly chat.

Lessons learned through silly schemes,
Awake in laughter, living dreams.
Balancing deep thoughts atop,
While giggles spill and never stop.

Every stumble, a new delight,
Discovering truths in the twilight.
With a wink, the world feels right,
As laughter guides us through the night.

Whirling with Whimsy

Spinning round like a top in glee,
Wisdom hides in absurdity.
With each twirl, I lose my way,
Found in folly's bright ballet.

Bubbles burst with ancient lore,
Laughter opens every door.
Ticklish truths in playful jest,
Life's little quirks are truly best.

I trip on thoughts that make me grin,
With each laugh, a new spin begins.
As whimsy wraps around the mind,
I dance and stretch, new joy to find.

The Lightness of Wisdom Unraveled

Cracking jokes with the wise and old,
Turns out wisdom's quite bold.
A tickle here, a pun there,
Unraveling truths with playful flair.

In moments bright, a chuckle's grace,
Each giggle brings a warm embrace.
Serious thoughts fall to the floor,
Who knew wisdom could be a chore?

Layers peel with silly wit,
Wrapped in laughter, never quit.
Finding depth in playful air,
Wisdom waits; we walk with flare.

Embracing Life's Playful Mysteries

Juggling questions, tossing doubts,
In a circus of twists and shouts.
Life's a riddle wrapped in laughs,
Finding truth in silly paths.

Every mystery hides a jest,
Who knew play could be the best?
In each surprise, a giggle glows,
Unlocking joy that truly flows.

Embracing quirks, we learn to see,
The secrets wrapped in jubilee.
In this dance of wisdom bright,
We twirl together, hearts in flight.

Dancing on the Edge of Enlightenment

In a world of riddles, I prance and twirl,
With a grin so wide, my thoughts unfurl.
Every misstep, a giggle, a grace,
I chuckle at shadows, and they lose their place.

Jumps like a rubber band, mind in flight,
Chasing the sunshine, avoiding the fright.
Questions like confetti, they scatter and spread,
With laughter as wisdom, I hop out of bed.

The Bright Side of the Infinite

Stars wink at me, they're in on the joke,
The more I ponder, the more I poke.
Galaxies giggle, planets align,
Tickling my soul, oh divine design!

Cosmic chuckles echo through space,
Life on the edge, oh what a race!
Twirling with stardust, I spin and I sway,
Discovering joy in the silliest way.

Tickle me, Oh Universe

With each cosmic nudge, I burst into glee,
The universe winks, as if to agree.
Questions like tickles, light up my mind,
Chasing the laughter, I leave doubt behind.

From black holes to bubbles, all things collide,
In this zany dance, let humor be my guide.
Sparks of delight, in every small thing,
Awakening joy that makes my heart sing.

Humor's Dance with the Divine

In a giggly waltz, I twine with the fate,
With puns like petals, we dance and create.
Twirling through truths that tickle the soul,
Reveling in moments, that's my ultimate goal.

The sacred is silly, a jest in disguise,
With each playful poke, I open my eyes.
Joy weaves a tapestry, vibrant and bright,
In the arms of the cosmos, I celebrate light.

The Chorus of Chuckles

In a room filled with giggles, so bright,
Laughter dances like stars in the night.
Tickles and snickers, a delightful spree,
Who knew wisdom was this carefree?

Bubbles of joy, they bounce all around,
Each chuckle a treasure, a joy to be found.
Whispers of humor, such sweet serenade,
In the song of the silly, our worries do fade.

A tumble, a stumble, a slip on the floor,
Each pop of a joke, we come back for more.
Laughter the potion, it lifts our old frown,
A symphony played in this whimsical town.

Comedic revelations, like flowers in bloom,
In the garden of giggles, we banish all gloom.
Together we chuckle, in a joyful parade,
In the chorus of laughter, our worries are laid.

Heartbeats in a Joyful Accord

With a wink and a nod, our spirits ignite,
Jokes in the air, everything feels right.
Ticklish thoughts pirouette with delight,
In the rhythm of mirth, our hearts take flight.

A wobble, a giggle, the globe goes round,
In this dance of the foolish, true joy is found.
Stories spun silly, like threads of pure gold,
In the fabric of laughter, we all brave and bold.

Echoes of humor, like whispers of spring,
Bring out the lightness, oh joy it can bring.
With each hearty chuckle, we heal and we mend,
In the pulse of the playful, all hearts can blend.

Jumping to joy with a skip and a sway,
Life's sweetest lessons are rife with the play.
In this heartbeat of giggles, we rise and we soar,
In the dance of pure mirth, forever wanting more.

Wisdom Wrapped in Laughter's Embrace

In the glimmer of jokes, profound truths arise,
Wrapped in the giggles, a strange sweet surprise.
Each snort and each howl opens up the way,
To wisdom that shines brightly, come what may.

Through merry mishaps and strange little tales,
Life's greatest lessons ride on humor's sails.
With a wink and a grin, all burdens are shed,
In the comedy chaos, we laugh instead.

The punchlines of life hit just right on cue,
Every chuckle creates something new.
A tickled reflection in life's goofy glass,
In the laughter we share, the moments can last.

So come join the circus, let joy be our guide,
With each burst of laughter, nothing can hide.
In the wisdom of jesters, true joy we will find,
Wrapped in their laughter, the heart and the mind.

Synchronized with the Sound of Joy

In the playground of giggles, our spirits collide,
With jests flying high, we take life in stride.
Chimes of delight ring out in the sun,
With giggles together, we feel we've won.

Prancing on dreams, with jokes in our pockets,
Chortles and chuckles, our hearts in the sockets.
We twirl through the punchlines, cascading with glee,
Each gleeful note sings sweet harmony.

In the symphony of smiles, we dance in our shoes,
Every whim brings us closer, we've nothing to lose.
A riddle, a pun, and our worries take flight,
In laughter's embrace, the world feels just right.

So come take a seat, join the joyfully loud,
In the music of laughter, we're always so proud.
In this rhythm of wonder, let us just sway,
Synchronized together in the sound of our play.

Fables of Frivolity and Insight

A jester prances, bright and bold,
With tales of wisdom, fun to behold.
In laughter's echoes, lessons creep,
As silly stories gently seep.

A wise old owl, in feathers fine,
Speaks riddles wrapped in punchline.
With each chuckle, an insight glows,
Through folly's door, the truth then flows.

The cat with boots, a suitor's guise,
Chases the truth with gleaming eyes.
In mischief's dance, we find our way,
Through playful jest, we seize the day.

So heed the tales of whimsy spun,
For light and laughter are never done.
In folly's arms, wisdom takes flight,
As joy and insight spark the night.

Sweet Chaos of Understanding

A monkey swings from branch to branch,
While wisdom hides in every chance.
With silly tricks and playful schemes,
Life's mysteries unfold like dreams.

In messy kitchens full of cheer,
Cooking lessons blend with beer.
Stirring chaos with a wink,
Found truths in every clumsy clink.

The pie that falls, the cat that slips,
Bring giggles forth from would-be gripes.
Through topsy-turvy, we can glean,
A deeper truth in every scene.

So dance with folly like a friend,
In sweet confusion, worlds will bend.
A hearty laugh, a burst of light,
In chaos sweet, we find our sight.

The Dance of Revelatory Whimsy

Beneath a moonlit, starry night,
A rabbit twirls in sheer delight.
With every hop and jolly jig,
It spins the truths both grand and big.

A squirrel whispers soft and low,
In playful jest, wise words will flow.
When folly dances with the wise,
The heart expands, the spirit flies.

In wobbly steps, we seek to rhyme,
Finding wisdom lost in time.
A tug, a laugh, a nudge, a cheer,
Through playful glances, truth draws near.

Join in the frolic, dance around,
In whimsy's groove, insights abound.
With every chuckle and every spin,
Discovering joy, let life begin.

Smiles Beneath the Surface

A puddle splashes, kids at play,
Where smiles bloom in bright array.
With every ripple, laughter rings,
Underneath, the joy it brings.

The clown in town, with silly face,
Turns somber frowns to pure embrace.
In every gag, a truth emerges,
Transforming lives, the spirit surges.

The silly hats, the pranks galore,
Unlocking doors to wisdom's core.
In playful jests, deep thoughts arise,
Wrapped in giggles, no disguise.

So wear a grin, and share a jest,
In laughter's warmth, we feel the best.
Beneath the surface, smiles remain,
As joy and insight intertwine like rain.

The Ripple Effect of a Smile

A grin goes round like a bouncy ball,
Spreading joy, it captivates all.
Like sunshine breaking through a cloud,
In a room, it gathers the crowd.

Tickles tickle, laughter spills,
Even the grumpiest find thrills.
From one to two, then three to four,
A chuckle's worth so much more.

Frolic in the light of mirth,
Humor's magic gives life worth.
In a giggle, wisdom blooms,
Chasing away the creeping glooms.

The Joyful Journey Inward

Wander down the trail of fun,
With every pun, enlightenment's spun.
Through silly hats and absurd pranks,
Discover truth in merry flanks.

Each twist and turn, a laugh unfolds,
In playful jest, the heart beholds.
With each clown's wig and colored socks,
A dash of joy unlocks the locks.

Dancing through the fields of cheer,
A bumpy ride with friends so dear.
A jest is gold, a giggle's grace,
In this vast world, we find our place.

Epiphanies Through Cackles

In the midst of hearty peal,
A flash of truth, a tiny reel.
With every snicker, insight glows,
As wisdom sprouts from friendly foals.

The silliest thoughts can break the ice,
As laughter spills, it's quite precise.
From belly rolls to snorts so loud,
Enlightenment stands, proudly bowed.

Between the jokes and joyful cheer,
The answers rise, at last, appear.
Cackles bring clarity to mind,
In the humor, answers unwind.

Every Giggle a Step Closer

With each small laugh, the heart expands,
A journey paved with playful strands.
In every snort, a little leap,
Toward the truth we long to keep.

A chuckle here, a wink and grin,
With silly tales, we find within.
In jests and jibes, the light unveils,
New paths emerge, where laughter trails.

Every giggle dances bright,
Guiding us through the starry night.
In the fun, we find our way,
Closer to joy, come what may.

Whispers of Wisdom in Laughter

In shadows where the giggles roam,
Tiny truths begin to foam.
A chuckle here, a snicker there,
Life's quirks caught unaware.

Beneath the clouds of serious frowns,
A carnival of joy abounds.
With every smirk, the wisdom grows,
Like petals blooming from our woes.

We stumble and trip on the cosmic stage,
Gracefully foolish, we turn the page.
The universe grins, a shared delight,
As we dance through the silly night.

So let the laughter ring so true,
In giggles' embrace, we learn anew.
Each whisper of joy is wisdom's art,
A playful jolt to the heavy heart.

The Smile that Breaks the Darkness

When night creeps in with its heavy sighs,
A twinkle of joy ignites the skies.
A grin appears, spreading far and wide,
Warding off shadows, our trusty guide.

A joke is told with a winking eye,
Brightening corners where moody thoughts lie.
With each hearty chuckle, light will seep,
Chasing the gloom and waking the deep.

Foolish shenanigans, absurd and bright,
Battle the sorrows that haunt the night.
In the warmth of laughter, we find our way,
Emerging victorious, come what may.

A smile is a beacon, so bold and clear,
Guiding us onward, it's the path we cheer.
In this goofy journey, we all partake,
Finding the light in the jokes we make.

Grinning at the Universe

With a twinkle in my eye, I gaze above,
At a cosmos that plays, like a feathered dove.
Stars wink back, in a whimsical dance,
Inviting me closer to join the prance.

Every quirky moment, a cosmic jest,
Galaxies giggling, a grand little test.
I chuckle at fate as it scampers around,
In this comical chaos, joy is found.

A nod to the absurd, I tip my hat,
To the universe's humor, elegant and sprat.
From meteors flying to planets that spin,
It's all a big joke, and I'm here to grin.

So let's embrace laughter, no need for the frown,
As we bask in the light, let go of the crown.
Grinning at worlds, both near and afar,
Together we twirl, just as we are.

Humorous Paths to Truth

Through the forest of giggles, I wander free,
Over trees of laughter, under skies filled with glee.
Every stumble a lesson, each trip a clue,
The truths whisper softly, while I just pursue.

In the game of life, a jesting delight,
Wit and whimsy, my guiding light.
With each hearty laugh, barriers fall,
A collision of joy, uniting us all.

The roads may be bumpy, and the maps may fade,
Yet humor's a compass, a light in the shade.
Finding the blessings in tricks life can play,
With laughter, I dance on this quirky ballet.

Embrace the absurd, let the smiles unfold,
In this carnival of stories, both new and old.
Truth does often wear a playful guise,
And wisdom reveals through the sparkle of eyes.

Reveling in the Absurd

In a world of jumbled thoughts,
Socks mismatched, oh what a lot!
Curly mustaches worn with pride,
Sipping soup on a rollercoaster ride.

Jesters dance on hidden strings,
Trading wisdom for silly things.
Chasing butterflies with a net,
In the game of life, it's a safe bet.

Bananas smile from fruit bowls high,
As penguins ponder, oh me, oh my!
The clock ticks backward, time stands still,
And laughter slips in, a gentle thrill.

So let us feast on eccentric dreams,
For joy is found in the silliest schemes.
With open hearts and minds set free,
We dance with absurdity, glee to be.

Playful Echoes of the Soul

A tuba honks in the morning sun,
Chasing giggles, oh what fun!
Kites are flying, grand and bright,
Tickling clouds with pure delight.

Noses painted like rainbow fish,
Conversations that swish and swish.
Wiggle, wobble, twirl in glee,
The soul sings sweetly, can you see?

With every silly face we make,
Laughter bubbles, never fake.
Hopscotch dreams on pavement grays,
In simple joys, the heart will blaze.

So join the dance, don't be shy,
Let echoes of fun fill the sky.
For the soul's delight is bright and bold,
In playful moments, treasures unfold.

Radiance in the Ripple of Laughter

Bubbles float in a sunlit breeze,
Twirling thoughts, as light as leaves.
A puppy chasing its own tail,
Wagging joy in a never-fail.

Tickle fights and glimmering eyes,
Upside-down cupcakes, oh what a prize!
Silly hats on every head,
In the dance of wit, we're all well-fed.

Chasing shadows that laugh and play,
Turning frowns into a bright bouquet.
Every chuckle, a spark of gold,
In laughter's embrace, we're brave and bold.

So let the giggles ripple wide,
In every heart, let humor reside.
With radiance found in mirth's sweet glow,
A journey of wonder, let's happily go.

The Sweetness of Serendipity

Stumbling upon a slice of pie,
With a grin and a twinkle, oh my!
Serendipity wraps in marshmallow dreams,
Where reality's better than it seems.

Bouncing off walls, carefree delight,
The world's a stage, and what a sight!
Kaleidoscope laughter fills the air,
Every moment is a breath of flair.

Coffee spills and giggles fly,
Conversations that twist and tie.
With a wink and a nudge, we swoop and glide,
In the joy of surprise, we happily ride.

So savor each quirky twist of fate,
With every stumble, we elevate.
The sweetness found in life's great spree,
Is simply a dance with serendipity.

Radiance Found in Light-Hearted Moments

In sunshine's glow, we dance so bright,
Tickles of joy in morning's light.
The silly sounds that fill the air,
Bring grins and giggles everywhere.

With playful pranks and friendly jests,
We find our peace in simple quests.
Laughter bubbles like a stream,
A joyful heart, a sparkling dream.

Clouds drift by, they make us grin,
With every chuckle, we begin.
In moments shared, our spirits soar,
The light-hearted can ask for more.

The world grows bright with each delight,
In every laugh, we find the light.
A joyous journey, pure and true,
Together, we seek the fun anew.

Echoes of Joy Through Time

A tickle here, a joke well-placed,
Through winding paths, our smiles embraced.
The giggles echo, soft and free,
In moments shared, just you and me.

Ticklish tales from days of yore,
Carry laughter from shore to shore.
As we reminisce, we find our rhyme,
In silly seconds, we conquer time.

The shadows dance, the spirits play,
With every chuckle, we seize the day.
Life's quirks whisper in our ear,
Reminding us of joy so near.

Through twilight hours, our voices blend,
In playful banter, hearts transcend.
With laughter woven through our days,
We embrace joy in countless ways.

Tickled by the Universe

Stars twinkle like a jester's grin,
Winking down as the fun begins.
The cosmos laughs in cosmic glee,
As I spin round in dizzy spree.

Each comet's tail, a feathered tease,
Galaxies giggle in gentle breeze.
The moon joins in with a cheeky smile,
While planets dance in carefree style.

In the galaxy's arms, we float and sway,
Tickled by secrets the stars convey.
With every wink, a spark ignites,
In the vastness, we find delights.

Like cosmic jesters, the stars align,
In their laughter, our spirits dine.
In this vast, playful, starry sea,
We find our joy, just you and me.

A Journey Through Ticklish Thoughts

In the maze of my mind, funny thoughts collide,
As giggles and smirks take us for a ride.
With memories like confetti in the air,
Each one a sparkle, beyond compare.

What if clouds wore fuzzy socks one day?
Or if squirrels sang and danced in play?
Each ticklish thought brings a smile to my face,
In the carnival of laughter, a joyful space.

Along the path, my worries slip away,
With a skip, a hop, in this grand display.
Every chuckle echoes through the trees,
In this whimsical world, I float with ease.

So let's wander through these ticklish dreams,
Where nothing is serious, or so it seems.
With hearts light and merry, we'll sail along,
In the comfort of laughter, we all belong.

Witty Whispers of the Divine

In the garden of jest, blooms divine,
Where giggles entwine with sacred sign.
The cosmos chuckles, stars wink bright,
In every joke, there's a sliver of light.

Silly sages dance on the breeze,
With puns that float like autumn leaves.
The universe grins, a prankster's delight,
Leading us slowly through the night.

Beneath the sky, laughter takes flight,
Tickling hearts, igniting the night.
In playful rhythms, we find the truth,
Chasing shadows of forgotten youth.

Each giggle a guide, each chuckle a clue,
The divine's in the punchline, oh, who knew?
With a smirk from above, we twirl and sway,
In this cosmic jest, we've lost our way.

Finding Peace in Punchlines

Witty quips like breezes blow,
In the chaos of life, they steal the show.
Every tickle of truth wraps me tight,
Swaddled in laughter, everything feels right.

Comic tales danced on the tongue,
Filling the world where complaints once hung.
With each teasing jest, we melt the strife,
Finding calm in the rhythm of life.

Banana peels on a serious day,
Trip me into joy, lead me astray.
In the punchlines spoken, I find my grace,
A moment of stillness in this mad race.

With each hearty chuckle, worries fade,
In humor's embrace, my fears cascaded.
From fumbles and flops, a lesson does bloom,
In the laughter's wake, all darkness is doomed.

The Hilarity of Being

Life's a circus of clowns in disguise,
With cotton candy dreams and pie-in-the-eye.
Each pratfall a lesson, each joke a blink,
In the shadowy corners, we chuckle and think.

Tangled in joy, we flip and we spin,
Finding grace in the chaos where chaos begins.
The world's a stage, with roles we all play,
In the script of existence, we find our own way.

Silly quirks wrapped in a gleeful cheer,
Reminding us gently, we need not fear.
With a wink from the cosmos, we stroll hand in hand,
In this playful dance of the grand cosmic band.

Jesting with life, oh what a delight,
Turning the mundane into purest insight.
In the laughter we share, our spirits take wing,
Reveling in the hilarity that existence can bring.

Riddles Wrapped in Joy

In a riddle wrapped, I find my way,
With giggles and grins, I seize the day.
What am I? A leap, a bound, or a fall?
A question of laughter that beckons us all.

Jokes as treasures, we seek and we find,
With a snicker and smile, we're beautifully blind.
What tickles the spirit, makes worries depart?
A punchline revealed, a turn of the heart.

Inside every quirk, a riddle does lie,
Sprinkled with joy, it can't help but fly.
In each wink of fate, in each playful jest,
We unwrap the mystery, we're truly blessed.

So dance with the whimsy, embrace the odd,
In riddles of joy, we laugh with the god.
Each chuckle a spark, igniting the air,
In this world of laughter, we lounge without care.

Mirth as a Mirror to the Soul

In shadows deep, a jest takes flight,
With giggles echoing through the night.
Reflections dance upon the walls,
Each chuckle bursting like bright balloons.

A hearty guffaw, a playful tease,
Life's absurdities bend with ease.
Take the time to share a grin,
Let silliness draw you from within.

The twinkle in the eye shines bright,
Beneath the laughter, wisdom's light.
For joy and folly often blend,
In every joke, a truth we send.

Mirth—a mirror, a guide for all,
In every stumble, we rise or fall.
So let your spirit soar and twirl,
Embrace the silliness of the world.

Serene Smiles Under Starlit Skies

Beneath the stars, we share our dreams,
Each chuckle floats on midnight beams.
The universe winked with delight,
As we crammed joy into the night.

With playful banter, we exchanged,
The cosmos laughed, no need for change.
In every jest, the heavens sway,
They twinkled back, 'Just be, just play.'

Our laughter danced on winds so free,
As gentle as a drifting sea.
With every chuckle, we align,
Finding peace where stars entwine.

So here we sit, 'neath velvet skies,
With grinning hearts and sparkling eyes.
In cosmic humor, truths unfold,
Serene and bright, our souls behold.

The Enlightenment of a Grinning Heart

With every smile, a spark ignites,
A journey starts with joyful heights.
In playful moments, wisdom thrives,
A heart that grins, forever thrives.

Tickled thoughts dance through our minds,
As laughter weaves what truth unwinds.
The world transforms when light prevails,
In joyful hearts, enlightenment hails.

Finding bliss in every jest,
And knowing life is but a quest.
Through silly tales, we navigate,
A grinning heart can never wait.

So let us laugh, deny the frown,
With playful spirits, we wear the crown.
In kindness wrapped and humor spun,
A grinning heart has already won.

Joyful Reflections on a Quiet Lake

On tranquil waters, ripples play,
As laughter whispers through the day.
With every splash, reflections bloom,
Creating joy that fills the room.

Beneath the surface, secrets flow,
Each chuckle stirs what we don't know.
Life's nuances, a comical game,
In sparkling ripples, we find the same.

Paddling forth with lightened hearts,
Every giggle, an art that starts.
The mirror lake reflects our glee,
In playful chaos, we're truly free.

So cast your worries, let them glide,
In the silent depths, let joy reside.
For in each ripple and every laugh,
We discover life's true aftermath.

Whimsy Above the Worries

In the garden where giggles bloom,
A butterfly danced, dispelling gloom.
With each flutter, worries take flight,
Chasing shadows with pure delight.

Clouds of frown drift far away,
As squirrels plan a silly play.
Tickling the air with joyful sounds,
In laughter, true freedom abounds.

The sun throws a wink at the trees,
While flowers sway in a teasing breeze.
Glee is the compass in this bright space,
Worries dissolve without a trace.

So let whimsies sprinkle your day,
In every corner, let joy have its say.
For in the dance of delight, we see,
The magic that sets every heart free.

The Healing Power of Chuckles

A giggle can heal like a warm embrace,
Turning frowns into a smiling face.
With every chuckle, a burden drops,
Life's troubles are mere hiccup stops.

In a world where the serious roam,
Find a jester, make their laugh your home.
Each snicker a step toward wholeness near,
Each snort a promise, bliss is here.

Ticklish tales shared under the moon,
Joy in jest, a delightful tune.
Let the belly laughs echo loud,
Join the foolish, be cheerful and proud.

So gather around for a hearty cheer,
Let silliness wash away every fear.
For this alchemy, a precious gold,
In chuckles, the universe unfolds.

Curiosity in a Burst of Laughter

Curiosity dances on a puppet thread,
With every giggle, new journeys spread.
What if we peeked into a clown's heart?
Where whimsy and wonder play their part?

A tickled nose in a curious quest,
Discovering truths through a jester's jest.
Wandering down paths of giggling delight,
Curiosity shines in the starlit night.

Who knew that a banana peel's fall,
Could spark insights, like a wake-up call?
Each chuckle a key to unlock the mind,
In silliness, endless treasures we find.

So let the laughter lead us away,
Into the mysteries of life's ballet.
For in each belly laugh and glee,
Lies the magic of what we can be.

The Philosophy of Playfulness

In every whimsy, a lesson lurks,
In playful moments, wisdom works.
Dizzy spins on the merry-go-round,
Teach us truths that joy has found.

A giggle hides in the folds of strife,
Turning monotony into joyful life.
With each playful poke, reality bends,
In the lightness, true vision transcends.

Look closely, the world wears a bright grin,
In silliness, the wonders begin.
Philosophy wrapped in a frolicsome dance,
Invitation to take a rollicking chance.

So chuckle at shadows that loom so tall,
Embrace the mirth that unites us all.
For life is a canvas where laughter paints,
A picture of play where each heart faints.

Finding Serenity in Silliness

A duck in a hat, what a sight!
It waddles around, charming and bright.
Laughter bubbles like a stream,
Where the wildest thoughts dare to dream.

Frogs in tuxedos, dancing with flair,
Umbrellas in hands, without a care.
Each giggle unravels tight knots,
In stillness, we find joy in our spots.

Lollipops rain from the cotton candy sky,
We chase after whims, watching time fly.
With every chuckle, clouds disappear,
In silliness, there's nothing to fear.

So paint your world with colors bold,
In laughter, find treasures more precious than gold.
We sway to the rhythm of life's vibrant tune,
Finding peace in the light of a spoon.

The Path of Cheerful Wandering

Stumbling on rainbows, who knew it could be?
The joy of a journey where everything's free.
Each step keeps a beat, a light-hearted song,
In the dance of the silly, where we all belong.

Here come the clouds with a sprinkle of fun,
A splash of delight, and we're on the run.
Through fields of giggles, we skip and we sway,
Creating a mosaic of laughter each day.

Lost in the woods where the gnomes like to play,
Their jokes echo softly, brightening the way.
With each silly riddle, a smile comes alive,
On this path of cheer, we joyfully thrive.

So let's twirl through this playful parade,
In the garden of chuckles where memories are made.
Wandering freely, no maps to confine,
In the land of giggles, the stars brightly shine.

Revelations in a Fit of Giggles

In the midst of chaos, there's a spark,
A burst of pure joy in the dark.
Each ripple of laughter unveils a view,
Where truths come alive, colorful and new.

From ticklish whispers to playful sighs,
The universe chuckles, oh how it flies!
In fits of glee, wisdom takes flight,
With every hearty giggle, we shine so bright.

A teapot that sings with a melody sweet,
Inviting us over for a whimsical treat.
With each cup of mirth, we ponder and play,
Unlocking the secrets of life's funny way.

So let's leap into laughter, with hearts open wide,
For in moments of joy, our spirits collide.
The revelations dance like butterflies free,
In this wondrous fit of giggles, just you and me.

Harmony in the Dance of Laughter

The sun winks down, warming the ground,
In the sway of our smiles, love's magic is found.
We twirl like dervishes, light on our feet,
With giggles that echo, making life sweet.

A jester appears with a cat on a chair,
Telling tall tales while slipping on air.
Each chuckle they share, like music it plays,
Creating a rhythm, a bright sunny blaze.

In fields of daisies, joy takes the lead,
Laughter blooms gently, fulfilling the need.
With every twirl and every soft laugh,
We paint a portrait, a joyful epigraph.

So let's dance in the moonbeams, wild and free,
With laughter as our guide, as simple as three.
In harmony's embrace, we find our true place,
In this merry dance, we joyfully trace.

Contemplation in Cheerful Chaos

Amidst the chaos, I trip and fall,
Laughter erupts, it's a free-for-all.
In puddles of giggles, wisdom hides,
We wade through joy, where reason abides.

Thoughts like balloons, float up so high,
Chasing them down, I can't help but sigh.
Silly distractions, they tug at my mind,
In this mad dance, new truths I find.

Life's riddles wrapped in a clown's big shoes,
Wandering laughter, my favorite muse.
Each tumble sparks light, ignites my soul,
In mess and mirth, I become whole.

With chaotic glee, I sip my tea,
Spilling wisdom, oh, can't you see?
In the storm of giggles, the lessons pour,
Tripping on joy, who could want more?

Humor as Our Unseen Guide

In a jester's cap, I seek direction,
Fumbling my way to sweet connection.
With every chuckle, my path grows clear,
Mapping the world by the notes I hear.

Witty whispers float through the air,
Reminding me that fun is everywhere.
In the heart of the jest, life reveals,
The soft embrace of humor heals.

Behind every mishap, a punchline waits,
Tickling wisdom at the golden gates.
Sliding on laughter, I find my way,
To lessons hidden in lighthearted play.

So let the chuckles guide my steps,
Navigating life through joyous pep.
Each twist and turn, a chance to rejoice,
In the symphony of giggles, I find my voice.

The Celestial Dance of Delight

Stars waltz around in a cosmic spree,
Joking with planets, oh what glee!
Laughter reverberates through the night,
A joyful chorus in radiant flight.

The moon shows up in polka dots,
Trading glances with sunburnt spots.
Galaxies swirl in a happy trance,
Life's grand theater puts us in a dance.

Comets twirl with comedic flair,
Poking fun at our worries and care.
As we spin through the vast unknown,
Laughter's spark lights up our throne.

With each twinkle, a giggle ignites,
Connecting us all in the starry nights.
To the rhythm of joy, we sway and sway,
In this cosmic folly, we find our way.

Unravelling Threads of Joy

Each thread I pull is a poke in the ribs,
Stitched with laughter, adorned with quips.
As I unravel this tapestry bright,
Tangles of giggles come into sight.

Patterns emerging like chuckles in bloom,
Weaving wise tales in a colorful room.
With a wink and a nod, the fabric shifts,
Twirling my heart with whimsical lifts.

The kite of joy dances high in the sky,
Tugging on clouds that drift light and spry.
As I chase it down, with a skip and a hop,
I learn that true joy never will stop.

So here I stand, a thread in this weave,
Crafting my laughter, it's all I believe.
In the quilt of existence, I find my place,
Sewn tight with delight, in this wondrous space.

Sunlight Streaming Through Chuckles

A giggle bursts like morning light,
Chasing shadows from the night.
Laughter dances, free and bold,
In bright hues, a story told.

A tickle here, a wink over there,
We trot on clouds without a care.
In the garden where joy breeds,
Each chuckle plants a thousand seeds.

With every snort, a frown takes flight,
Levity breaks the morning's bite.
We frolic through the sun's warm glow,
Where silly tales are free to flow.

So let's embrace this silly spree,
As sunlight sparkles on the sea.
In laughter's hold, we find our muse,
A tapestry of joy we choose.

Radiant Revelations in the Ripples of Joy

Joy bubbles up like springtime streams,
In the pool of laughter, we find our dreams.
With a wink and a nudge, we light the way,
Turning clouds into cotton candy spray.

As snickers twirl in a dizzy waltz,
We embrace our quirks, flaws, and faults.
From slippery slopes to stumbles grand,
Each fall spins us with a helping hand.

Grins stretch wide, illuminating faces,
In a world dressed in silly embraces.
Each chuckle forms a shimmering thread,
Weaving this tapestry where fun is widespread.

Radiance flows from small moments found,
In every uproar, joy knows no bound.
So come, let us dip our toes in glee,
And uncover the treasure of our jubilee.

Chasing Joy in the Sunlight

With a hop and a skip, we dash about,
Chasing giggles, dancing without doubt.
The sun smiles down with a wink and cheer,
As we twirl under skies so clear.

Sideways glances and playful shouts,
We tumble through life, that's what it's about.
In the playground of heartbeats and grins,
We discover the joy that truly begins.

A ticklish breeze, a playful tease,
Together we soar with incredible ease.
Echoes of laughter fill the air,
As happiness spreads everywhere.

In the warmth of rays, we chase and play,
Finding bliss in the silliest way.
Each moment a spark, igniting the fun,
We wander as children, two souls become one.

Whispers of Humor in Sacred Spaces

In quiet places, laughter whispers soft,
A giggle sneaks as spirits loft.
Within the stillness, we hold a jest,
Where humor dances, feeling blessed.

Between the breaths of sacred thought,
We gather joy from what we've sought.
With a playful bard to guide our way,
Each chuckle brightens the break of day.

As shadows play on the chapel wall,
We roll in the aisles, into giggles we fall.
A secret shared, a knowing glance,
In every moment, we take a chance.

So in these spaces where we align,
Let humor purify, with love it twines.
In the echoes of laughter, harmony sings,
Joy springs eternal on gossamer wings.

Lighthearted Inspections of Existence

In a world of jumbled thoughts,
I tripped on my own shoes.
The universe, it giggles loud,
As I ponder what to choose.

Bananas slip with perfect grace,
While I dance in awkward glee.
All the wise folks scratch their heads,
What's the meaning of a tree?

I see a cloud that looks like me,
With a grin that brings delight.
A muddled heart, a goofy soul,
A brighter day—a silly sight.

With every question makes me laugh,
And ponder life's absurd ways.
The secrets hide in silly smiles,
A joke in cosmic plays.

The Soundtrack of Joyful Realizations

A melody of chuckles flows,
As I skip through life's parade.
Every mishap plays a note,
In this symphony, I wade.

I stumbled on a word today,
And it danced right out of sight.
The vibrant tunes of silly slips,
Bring a heart into the light.

Chasing shadows made of sound,
They jiggle when I sway.
The rhythm of delightful blunders,
Always leads me to play.

In a concert of joy, I find,
The laughter wraps around my mind.
With every giggle, wisdom stirs,
And in the fun, my spirit whirs.

Witty Wanderings to Clarity

I trod a path of riddles wide,
With a grin I jogged along.
Each twisty thought was dancing light,
Singing out a merry song.

I found a sign that said, 'Be bold!'
But the arrow pointed wrong.
Yet laughter filled my wayward steps,
As I joined the joyful throng.

Along the trail of quirky sights,
My doubts began to fade.
With every chuckle, bliss took flight,
In this frolic I had made.

A jester's hat, a heart of gold,
I seek the path of cheer.
In witty whims and silly thoughts,
True clarity draws near.

Serenity Found in Starlit Laughter

Beneath a sky of twinkling stars,
I counted laughs like sheep.
Each chuckle shot like starlight beams,
In silence, joy runs deep.

A firefly flits with silly grace,
While crickets hum their tune.
The universe, a playful muse,
Transforms the night to noon.

I muse on life with a sardonic grin,
As the cosmos whispers low.
Each giggle born from cosmic play,
In starry fields, we grow.

With every chuckle shared with friends,
A brighter path appears.
Serenity smiles on our hearts,
As laughter dries our tears.

The Comedy of Realization

In a world of jest, I skipped and danced,
Ideas turned into jokes, and I pranced.
With every stumble, wisdom slipped in,
Oh, the joy of truth wrapped in a grin!

I tripped over thoughts, just like my shoes,
Got lost in laughter, forgot to lose.
A punchline of life, so quirky and bright,
Each chuckle a star, lighting up the night.

With every belly laugh, I turned a page,
Found meaning in chaos, the world's stage.
Tickled by wisdom, with wit up my sleeve,
I learned to play and to truly believe.

So here's to the humor, in all that we see,
A comic adventure, just me and me.
In the circus of life, I found my place,
Wit and wisdom dancing in endless embrace.

Mirthful Steps on Sacred Ground

On this path of giggles, I wobbled with glee,
The grass tickled toes, just like a spree.
With shadows of laughter gathered 'round,
I frolicked in circles, no lost and found.

A stumble here, a fall there, a jest in the air,
Every misstep a song, a moment to share.
My heart did a cartwheel; the trees chimed in,
Nature's own laugh track, let the fun begin!

Feet shuffling softly on this sacred terrain,
Laughter like raindrops, washing off pain.
With each joyous hop, my spirit took flight,
The ground turned to clouds, I soared with delight.

So I dance through the meadows, let shadows run free,
Finding the sacred in each snicker and spree.
With giggles and grins, the universe spun,
On this mirthful journey, I'm never outdone.

Tickled by Transcendence

In moments of silence, the giggles ignite,
As I float on my thoughts, take off in flight.
The universe chuckles, while I spin and sway,
With each tickle of life, I drift far away.

With wisdom that dances under the stars,
Holy jokes echo like symphonic guitars.
A wink from the cosmos, a grin from the sun,
In this temple of laughter, I know I have won.

I traded my worries for whimsical views,
As light-hearted banter swept away blues.
With each wave of joy, a ripple of peace,
In the ocean of humor, my fears find release.

So here's to the journey, a path truly grand,
With chuckles cascading, like grains on the sand.
In the dance of existence, I bravely presist,
Tickled by wonder, in humor, I coexist.

Jests of the Mind's Awakening

When thoughts burst like bubbles, a riotous sound,
Awakening moments, both silly and profound.
Each quip a butterfly, fluttering so light,
In gardens of laughter, I take flight at night.

The mind plays its tricks, a jester's delight,
With laughs as my lantern, I wander the night.
Every thought a riddle, unraveling fast,
Finding truth in absurdity, a spell that's cast.

Chasing after giggles, the secrets unfold,
Stories of wisdom in jest that they told.
With humor my compass, I navigate space,
In this cosmic comedy, I find my place.

So bring on the chuckles, let joy be my guide,
In the circus of learning, I never hide.
Through pranks and through puns, revelations unbind,
A laughter-filled journey, awakening the mind.

The Playful Path to Truth

In the garden of smiles we roam,
With tickles and giggles, we call it home.
Chasing shadows of doubt with a jest,
Finding wisdom, we laugh, and we rest.

Jokes on the mind, they dance and sway,
Turning frowns upside down, come what may.
Truth wears a grin, a mischievous face,
In folly and fun, we find our place.

Like clowns on the tightrope, we wobbly glide,
Over the abyss where seriousness hides.
Each chuckle a step, a bounce on the beam,
In this playful journey, we joyfully dream.

Wisdom's a prankster, inviting the light,
While laughter sprinkles stars through the night.
In the circus of life, we all play our part,
With a giggle, we dance to the beat of the heart.

Glee as Our Spiritual Compass

Glee is the path, it's wide and bright,
Leading us onward, day and night.
With chuckles we steer through shadows and doubt,
In joy's warm embrace, we flip things about.

Silly singsongs lead us near,
To treasures of truth, let's give a cheer!
With each hearty laugh, we shake off the gloom,
While happiness blossoms, it lights up the room.

The compass spins wildly but ever so true,
Guided by giggles, we know what to do.
When we stumble and trip, we bounce right back,
For joy is our map, on this whimsical track.

Floating on laughter like clouds in the sky,
With hearts wide open, we flit and we fly.
The journey is grand, each moment a thrill,
With glee as our guide, let's climb every hill.

The Heart's Unfolding Laughter

A heart full of laughter, a sight to behold,
Each giggle a treasure, each chuckle pure gold.
In the silence of smiles, wisdom unfolds,
As joy's gentle rhythm in stories is told.

Whispers of mirth in the soft morning air,
Life's little blunders become joys we can share.
With twinkles in eyes, we dance on the breeze,
Finding light in the shadows, we do as we please.

Let's tickle the cosmos and spin the stars bright,
With laughter as fuel, we lift to new heights.
The heart's joyful murmur, a melody sweet,
As we leap through existence on mirthful repeat.

In the garden of giggles, we tend to our soul,
With each hearty laugh, we emerge, we are whole.
From the depths of our being, let joyousness bloom,
For laughter unveils the heart's sacred room.

Treading Lightly Toward Clarity

With a hop, skip, and giggle, we wander the day,
Carrying joy in a frolicsome way.
Mistakes become stories that dance on our lips,
As we walk through the chaos and relish the trips.

With merriment guiding, we tread ever light,
Finding gems of insight in the fun and delight.
Each stumble a chance to let laughter take flight,
In the tapestry woven with threads oh so bright.

Through puddles of laughter, we splash as we go,
Collecting the moments that shimmer and glow.
With clarity blooming, like flowers in spring,
We find peace in the joy that each new day brings.

So let's chase the mirth where the wild meadows play,
For the path leads to wisdom in its quirky ballet.
In the dance of existence, with joy as our guide,
We discover the truths that quietly reside.

Humor as a Sacred Embrace

In the dance of daily plight,
We find a spark of silly light.
With giggles wrapped in soft embrace,
We stroll through life, a joyful race.

A chuckle here, a snicker there,
Transforms the weight we often bear.
In every blunder, there's a clue,
That life's a joke that's meant for two.

So lift your smile and let it show,
In every shadow, let it glow.
For in each laugh, a truth does swell,
That life is grand, and all is well.

Sipping Serenity with a Smile

With every sip of morning brew,
A playful thought comes rushing through.
The steam that curls up to the sky,
Whispers secrets, oh so spry.

As sunlight beams through kitchen panes,
We giggle at our morning gains.
Each moment sipped is pure delight,
Turning mundane into sheer bright.

With laughter bubbling in our cup,
We toast to life, we lift it up.
For serenity is but a grin,
That radiates from deep within.

Unraveling Truths Through Laughter

When life feels tight, a twist and turn,
We find a way to laugh and learn.
In silly faces, wisdom hides,
Like playful dolphins in the tides.

A chuckle cracks the heavy shell,
Revealing truths we know so well.
Through jests and jibes, we peel away,
The layers that distress our play.

With every giggle, we draw near,
To understanding, sweet and clear.
In every pun, a lesson lies,
A joy-filled path that always flies.

The Elixir of Joyful Realization

In the garden of our thoughts, we play,
With laughter sprouting, come what may.
Each jest a potion, bright and bold,
Unveiling stories yet untold.

As life hands us its wildest schemes,
We sip our dreams from joyful streams.
With every hearty laugh we share,
We find reflections everywhere.

So let the elixirs flow and swirl,
In playful moments, joy unfurl.
For through each chuckle, life's revealed,
In laughter's arms, our hearts are healed.

www.ingramcontent.com/pod-product-compliance
Lightning Source LLC
Chambersburg PA
CBHW051655160426
43209CB00004B/904